The BATHROOM TRIVIA DIGEST

———— • ————

Russ Edwards
Jack Kreismer

RED-LETTER PRESS, INC.
Saddle River, New Jersey

THE BATHROOM TRIVIA DIGEST
Revised and Updated 2010
Copyright © 2008 Red-Letter Press, Inc.
ISBN-10: 1-60387-102-0
ISBN-13: 978-1-60387-102-0

Red-Letter Press, Inc.
P.O. Box 393
Saddle River, NJ 07458
www.Red-LetterPress.com

ACKNOWLEDGEMENTS

EDITORIAL:

Jeff Kreismer & Kobus Reyneke

•

TYPOGRAPHY:

Christina Chybinski & Matt Taets

•

COVER:

Cliff Behum

•

SPECIAL MENTION:

Diana "Nana" Charshafian
Rita Kubran
The Sanibel Scullers

The
BATHROOM
TRIVIA DIGEST

———— • ————

Research shows that up to 40% of all people who come to your house for a party will snoop inside your medicine cabinet.

•

Roughly half of all the water in the earth's oceans is in the Pacific Ocean.

•

Despite credit on the labels, Elvis did not write nor co-write any of his songs.

•

Ole Bentzen, a Danish physician who may have thought that laughter was the best medicine, nonetheless overdosed on it while watching the film *A Fish Called Wanda* in 1989. He laughed so hard, his heart rate jumped to 500 beats a minute, causing him to die of a heart attack.

•

Coral is so similar to human bone, it is being used to replace bone grafts.

•

Blood makes up about seven percent of your body's weight.

•

If a month starts on a Sunday, it will have a Friday the 13th in it.

GRAFFITI

IF ALL IS NOT LOST, WHERE IS IT?

B.F. Goodrich coined the term "zipper." Until then, they had been called "separable fasteners."

•

Dalmatian puppies are born without any spots.

•

Studies reveal that the average American can read about 230 words per minute. Bill Gates reportedly makes an estimated 250 dollars a second. Assuming that you have average reading speed, in the time it takes you to read this, Mr. Gates will have earned approximately 3,000 dollars.

•

If Charles Lindbergh's grandfather hadn't changed the family's last name, the famed flier would have been known as Charles Manson.

•

Banana peels make excellent fertilizer for rose bushes.

•

Despite its name, the black bear can actually be chocolate, white, blonde or cinnamon in color.

•

The country's first drive-up window was installed by the Merchants Bank of Syracuse, NY in 1941.

THOUGHTS OF THE THRONE

On an episode of TV's "Married...with Children", main character Al Bundy constructed his ideal bathroom, which included five rolls of toilet paper and no sink.

Although we can't answer the perennial question of "Why did the chicken cross the road?" we can say that if it did, its top speed would be about 9 m.p.h.

•

Regis Philbin holds the record for being in front of TV cameras the longest.

•

Whales not only communicate, they speak in dialects.

•

The first paper money in the U.S. was issued by the Treasury in 1862 in an effort to finance the Civil War.

•

Superman was created by a Canadian.

•

At any given time, a Great White shark is packing around 3,000 teeth.

•

Tonsurphobia is a fear of haircuts.

•

Beware if you're on the road – There are 450,000,000 chickens in the U.S.

GRAFFITI

UNEMPLOYMENT ISN'T WORKING.

Cats can see about six times better than humans.

•

You may not know Nils Bohli but you surely know his invention –
the modern three point seatbelt.

•

In 1985, a buyer paid well over $200,000 for a bottle of 1787
Chateau Lafitte claret engraved with the initials of Thomas
Jefferson. About a year later, the cork dried out and turned it into
the most expensive vinegar of all time.

•

Nearly half of all notes printed by the Bureau of Engraving and
Printing are one-dollar bills.

•

Florida stretches across two time zones.

•

Israeli postage stamp glue is certified kosher.

•

If you live in Los Angeles and want to pop up to Reno for a bit of
action on the gaming tables, you'll have to head west.

•

The only Great Lake Michigan doesn't border on is Lake Ontario.

GRAFFITI

GETTING SICK AT AIRPORT
IS TERMINAL ILLNESS.

Bic pens were originally to be named after inventor Marcel Bich but marketers changed their minds and dropped the "h" when they thought about how the name might be pronounced in America.

•

George Clooney started acting in 1982 when his cousin, Miguel Ferrer (son of Rosemary Clooney and Jose Ferrer) wangled him a bit part in a movie. After that, he moved to Los Angeles to pursue a career in acting. He spent a year sleeping in a friend's closet but he eventually did all right for himself.

•

The first "modern" cell phone to have the public lined up around the block was the Motorola DynaTAC 8000X, otherwise known as "The Brick." It came out in 1984, weighed 2 pounds, only got a half hour of talk out of a recharge and cost nearly $4,000.

•

If anyone's looking for a Christmas gift for Santa, a tanning booth may be a good idea. At the North Pole, the sun stays below the horizon 186 days a year.

•

The happy little boy on cans of Play-Doh is known as Play-Doh Pete.

QUICK QUIZ

What's the only animal that's eaten
before it is born and after it is dead?

A chicken.

Nepal is the only nation without a rectangular flag.

•

A Canadian quarter carries the image of a caribou.

•

In Tennessee, it's illegal to drive while asleep.

•

Silly Putty was originally used as caulking compound.

•

If you're not doing anything next December 23rd, head on down to Oaxaca, Mexico, for The Night Of The Radishes. The locals carve the Jack-O- Radishes and display them in the town square as part of a pre-Christmas celebration.

•

Almost 50% of U.S. citizens live in the Eastern Time Zone.

•

The largest tumbleweed ever recorded was 38 feet in diameter.

•

Play-Doh was originally used as wallpaper cleaner.

•

A squirrel's tail can be used as a parachute, enabling it to fall up to 100 feet without injury.

THOUGHTS OF THE THRONE

Studies show that the stall closest to the door in a public restroom is usually the cleanest and least-used.

The first traffic light ever was installed in Cleveland, Ohio, in 1914.

•

If you've ever dreamed of climbing Mt. Everest, better hurry- it's getting taller by about a half-an-inch to one inch every year.

•

You probably always thought it was the Spirit of 76, but an act of Congress declared bourbon the official spirit of the USA.

•

An irrational fear of wine is called Oenophobia.

•

Cats have as many as 245 bones before they fuse together. Maybe that's why dogs chase them so much.

•

The license plate on the Oscar Mayer Weinermobile is YUMMY.

•

There are as many Italians in Toronto, Canada, as in Venice, Italy.

•

If you go on a wine tasting tour in Utah, it is against the law to swallow the wine.

•

99% of the living space on earth is under the ocean.

GRAFFITI

IF THE NO. 2 PENCIL IS THE MOST POPULAR, HOW COME IT'S NOT NO. 1?

The state of Minnesota forbids crossing state lines with a duck on your head.

•

One-fifth of all the fresh water in the world is in the Great Lakes.

•

The first patent for chewing gum was issued to William F. Semple in 1869.

•

Every person has a tongue print as individual as fingerprints, so if you're going safecracking, wear gloves and resist the urge to lick the dial.

•

There are about 350 species of sharks. Less that 10% of these species have ever been involved in an attack on humans.

•

More than 90% of the trade between nations is carried by ship.

•

Florida has two rivers named Withlacoochee.

•

Sandra Bullock, Bruce Willis, Chevy Chase, Bill Cosby, Tom Arnold and Kris Kristofferson are all former bartenders.

GRAFFITI

A TOUPEE IS TOP SECRET.

People were much shorter in Revolutionary times. Doorways from that period barely offered five feet of clearance.

•

Jimi Hendrix's first major North American tour was as opening act for The Monkees.

•

The hibernating arctic ground squirrel has antifreeze in its blood and is thus the only mammal to be able to survive freezing temperatures.

•

A 2X4 is really 1-1/2" by 3-1/2".

•

William Herschel discovered the planet Uranus in 1781 and named it Georgium Sidium in honor of King George III of England. In 1850, it was renamed Uranus, thereby assuring snickers for generations to come.

•

Once a fixture on TV, the last cigarette commercial was shown on Johnny Carson's *Tonight Show* January 1st, 1971.

•

A good deal of Florida's air pollution comes from dust blowing in from Africa.

QUICK QUIZ

If you ran the entire course of 1,661,220 inches, what would you have just completed?

A marathon.

It's estimated that the world's libraries store more than 100 million original volumes; 24 million of those are in the U.S. Library of Congress alone.

•

The average cat consumes about 127,750 calories a year, nearly 28 times its own weight.

•

Johnson & Johnson began marketing the Band-Aid bandage in 1921.

•

Garnet Carter built the world's first miniature golf course on Lookout Mountain in Tennessee in 1927.

•

Actor Gene Wilder's birth name was Jerome Silberman.

•

Baseball and the bathroom: The lucky fan who retrieved Barry Bonds' record tying 755th career home run in 2007 was 33-year-old Adam Hughes – a plumber.

•

If you stretched out a single human DNA molecule, it would be 5 feet, 5 inches long.

•

The estimated age of the world's oldest crow is 118 years.

THOUGHTS OF THE THRONE

The Beatles' George Harrison had a toilet seat which played *Lucy in the Sky with Diamonds.*

PEZ is short for pfefferminz, the German word for "peppermint". PEZ dispensers with character heads have been pumping out the compact candies since 1952.

•

American civil servants paychecks are recycled to make toilet rolls. (Insert your own comment here.)

•

The *Price Is Right*, on the air consecutively since 1972, is TV's longest-running game show.

•

There are more than 43,252,003,274,489,856,000 possible positions for a Rubik's Cube.

•

The total weight of termites on earth exceeds the total weight of humans. Nevertheless, you never see a termite worried about dieting

•

Galileo sketched a design of the first ballpoint pen.

•

Every day, Americans use over five billion gallons of water to flush.

•

It's not exactly brain food but according to the American Association of College Stores, the number-one most popular on-campus snack is a pack of Oreo cookies.

GRAFFITI

WORK FAST - NOT HALF FAST.

There are three words in the English language which end in "ceed" – exceed, proceed and succeed.

•

One gallon of paint would cover 930 acres if you could spread the coat out to one nanometer thick. That's an area about the size of New York's Central Park.

•

Steve King, who rode a wave for one hour and 17 minutes, holds the world record for the longest surf ride- 7.6 miles.

•

Joey Chestnut set the world wiener-eating record in 2007 when he downed 66 hot dogs and buns in 12 minutes.

•

The Big Apple has almost a half billion dollars in outstanding parking fines.

•

If the doctor tells you that you are suffering from graphospasms and scrivener's palsy, don't worry, that's just his hundred-dollar way of informing you that you have writer's cramp.

GRAFFITI

WHAT DO YOU SAY WHEN GOD SNEEZES?

Boomer icons Janis Joplin, Jimi Hendrix, and Jim Morrison were all 27 when they died.

•

The USA has the highest rate of plastic surgery in the world, followed by Mexico.

•

According to CNN, America's favorite pastime is reading.

•

Peter Boyle, most famous for playing Frank Barone in *Everybody Loves Raymond*, was best man at John Lennon's wedding.

•

The top-selling wine is the United States is Chardonnay.

•

Most pencils in America have eraser tips. Most pencils in Europe do not.

•

You knew it was true. You could feel it. Every day is longer than the day before it- by about 55 billionths of a second.

•

It's estimated that over 15,000,000 Americans abuse prescription drugs. That's more than all the illegal drugs combined.

QUICK QUIZ

What product was originally called Little Short-Cake Fingers?

Twinkies.

Beachcombers beware! It's a federal rap to disturb a dead whale.

•

John Glenn was the oldest American to go into space – twice.

•

Jamie Foxx's birth name was Eric Bishop.

•

On March 29, 1848, for the first time in history, Niagara Falls stopped flowing. An ice jam above the rim of The Falls caused the water to stop.

•

In 1990, cleaning crews working on the Statue of Liberty removed 600 pounds of chewing gum.

•

Elvis Presley made his Las Vegas debut at the Frontier Hotel on April 22nd, 1956. He didn't go over well with the middle-aged crowd and was fired a week later.

•

In the first four months of 2007, golfer Jacqueline Gagne sank 10 holes-in-one. The odds of this happening are estimated to be 1 out of 670,000,000,000,000,000,000.

THOUGHTS OF THE THRONE

Leave It to Beaver was the first program to show a toilet on television. However, only the tank of the toilet was seen on the episode.

43% of all beer sold is consumed by just 10% of beer drinkers.

•

Americans gobble a half billion Twinkies each year.

•

President Franklin Roosevelt once forgot his dog Fala and left him behind on a remote Alaskan island. He taught the Navy to play "fetch" as he dispatched a destroyer to pick him up.

•

In his boxing days, Frank Sinatra was known as Marty O'Brien and he wasn't all that good-in fact back then, he was known as "Old Black and Blue Eyes".

•

The names of Popeye's four nephews are Pipeye, Peepeye, Pupeye, and Poopeye.

•

In terms of catastrophic spinal and head injuries, the one activity that is more dangerous than all other high school and college sports combined is cheerleading.

•

According to an Australian study, vegetarians were more intelligent than people who ate meat.

— GRAFFITI —

A WAIST IS A TERRIBLE THING TO MIND.

Dr Pepper was named after a real doctor in Virginia who gave the drink's inventor, Wade Morrison, his first job. By the way, there's no period after the "Dr" in Dr Pepper.

•

The daily heat output of the human body is enough to boil eight gallons of freezing water.

•

Pope John Paul II once hit #3 on the Polish Pop Charts- at least his poetry did, as it was set to a disco beat.

•

The only battle fought on American soil since the Civil War was the One Thousand Mile War in 1943, when Japan invaded the Aleutian Islands.

•

Among The Beatles, Paul McCartney and Ringo Starr were left-handed.

•

No winter Olympic medals have ever been won by African or South American countries.

•

In an average lifetime, a woman will consume six pounds of lipstick.

GRAFFITI

HOW COME "LISP" HAS AN "S" IN IT?

Pope John Paul II was once named an "Honorary Harlem Globetrotter".

•

There is a law in Rochester, Michigan, that anyone bathing in public must have their bathing suit inspected by a police officer. Apparently the town doesn't give people enough credit to tell right from thong.

•

Tom Cruise was born Thomas Mapother IV.

•

Beaver, Oklahoma, is known as the Cow Chip Throwing Capital of the World.

•

Sugar Ray Robinson was originally tagged with the moniker Walker Smith, Jr.

•

The presidential residence has only been known as "The White House" since 1901, when it was officially named so by Teddy Roosevelt.

•

In 2001, Utah became the first state to adopt an official state snack- Jell-O.

QUICK QUIZ

If you spell out numbers, how far can you get before you have to use the letter "a"?

666

One reason Bollywood is such a powerhouse of filmmaking is that Indians go to the movies over three billion times a year.

•

There are over 3,000 species of mosquitoes. That's a lot of blood-suckers even if you don't count politicians.

•

This may bug you but for every human being on earth, there are about 200 million insects.

•

University of Oregon student Carolyn Davidson designed the Nike logo in 1964. She was paid $35 for the design.

•

When they first started out, The Commodores, one of the most popular musical groups of the '70s, could not agree upon a name. One of the members said he was going to open a dictionary and another member had to blindly point to a word. Whatever it was, it would be their name. Lionel Ritchie was thus one word away from being frontman for "The Commodes."

•

A study done by the *Journal of the American Medical Association* found that 32% of studies are inaccurate.

THOUGHTS OF THE THRONE

*The first "Please don't squeeze the Charmin'"
toilet paper commercial was appropriately filmed
in Flushing, New York.*

SCUBA divers cannot pass gas below 33 feet.

•

Over his or her lifetime, the average person walks 115,000 miles.

•

Only about 20% of diamonds are made into jewels.

•

Your skin sheds 50,000 cells every minute.

•

Americans create about 1/5 of the world's garbage annually. That's about 3 pounds a day per person.

•

Karaoke means "empty orchestra" in Japanese.

•

At any given time, around 0.7% of the world's population is drunk.

•

If you ever wondered why Charlie Brown's hair was always like that, his father was a barber.

•

India has a Bill of Rights for cows. That comes in handy in case anybody has a beef.

GRAFFITI

WARS DON'T DECIDE WHO'S RIGHT,
ONLY WHO'S LEFT.

The average American spends 6 years of their life in the bathroom and only 6 months at stoplights. So which do you think involves more stop and go?

•

About 200,000,000 M&M's are sold each day in the USA.

•

On the very day Lincoln was assassinated, John Wilkes Booth stalked General Grant's wife, Julia. The Grants declined the invitation to go to Ford's Theater that evening and went instead to Burlington, New Jersey, to visit their children.

•

The second span of the Tacoma Narrows Bridge in Tacoma, Washington, opened in 2007. With a total length of 5,979 feet, it's the longest twin suspension bridge in the world.

•

It is estimated that there are over 50,000 professional Elvis impersonators. That's a lot of peanut butter and banana sandwiches.

•

There are 318,979,564,000 possible combinations of the first four moves in Chess.

GRAFFITI

HOW COME PHONETICS IS NOT
SPELLED THE WAY IT SOUNDS?

Until the 1960s, men with long hair were not allowed in Disneyland. Yeah, but they let Donald Duck run around the place with no pants.

•

It is estimated that 4 million "junk" telephone calls are made daily.

•

Despite a population of over a billion, China has only about 200 family names, so if you use the phone book, it's all too easy to Wing the Wong number.

•

Bananas can get "sunburned." The resulting dark brown or black spots look like, but are not necessarily, a sign of over-ripeness.

•

The only street in the world to claim two Nobel Peace Prize winners is in Soweto in South Africa. Nelson Mandela and Archbishop Desmond Tutu both have abodes in Vilakazi St., Orlando West.

•

The largest recorded pumpkin grown was certified at the Pennsylvania Giant Pumpkin Growers Weigh-Off in 2005. It weighed in at 1,469 pounds.

QUICK QUIZ

Who was the first Little Leaguer to become
President of the United States?

George W. Bush - Dubya played catcher as a Little Leaguer in Midland, Texas, from 1955 to 1958.

Pearls melt in vinegar. Watch out Mrs. Cleaver! Don't lean too far over that salad dressing.

•

The "umbrella girl" of the Morton Salt Company and her accompanying slogan – "When it rains, it pours," made their first appearance in 1911.

•

The biggest consumers of coffee in the world, per capita, are Finland, Sweden, Norway and Denmark.

•

About 20 to 30 volcanoes erupt each year, mostly under the sea.

•

In 1967, The Monkees outsold both The Beatles and The Stones.

•

In 1970, Diane Crump became the first female jockey in the Kentucky Derby.

•

In the sixteenth century, bread was portioned out by status. Laborers or servants got the burnt bottom of the loaf, the family got the middle, and guests enjoyed the top, or as we refer to them today, the "upper crust."

THOUGHTS OF THE THRONE

Green Bay, Wisconsin, claims to be
The Toilet Paper Capital of the World.

The eggplant is actually a berry.

•

Researchers at Purdue University reported that their licking machine, modeled after a human tongue, required an average of 364 licks to get to the center of a Tootsie Pop.

•

Up to 8% of men are deficient in color vision.

•

South Africa has the cheapest electricity in the world.

•

Both of James Madison's vice presidents died while in office.

•

On average, 90% of Dutch teenagers can speak English fluently.

•

Not just any corn can be popcorn. It requires a variety with extra moisture inside to generate the steam which causes the corn to pop.

•

When he graduated from West Point, Ulysses S. Grant had no intention of making the military his career and looked forward instead to a career as a professor of mathematics.

—— GRAFFITI ——

LIFE IS WONDERFUL.
WITHOUT IT YOU'D BE DEAD.

The most popular toothbrush color in America is blue.

•

In 1978, Janet Parker, a medical photographer, became the last person known to die of smallpox.

•

Actress Reese Witherspoon is a direct descendant of John Witherspoon, one of the 56 signers of the *Declaration of Independence.*

•

Pumpkins are actually a fruit.

•

St. Nicholas Church is located in Santa Claus, Indiana.

•

A cat has 18 toes, five on the front paws and four on the back.

•

An elephant can drink 15,000 gallons of water in one year.

•

Olivia and Elizabeth Norris were sisters. They married immigrants who began a small candle and soap business- that now has 135,000 employees in over 80 countries. Their names were William Proctor and James Gamble.

GRAFFITI

KINDRED IS THE FEAR THAT
YOUR RELATIVES ARE COMING.

Dogs and humans are the only animals with prostates. That probably explains why each species has a similar reaction to hearing the snap of a rubber glove.

•

The tallest monument in the U.S. is the 630-foot Jefferson National Expansion Memorial, also known as the Gateway Arch in St. Louis.

•

The International Olympic Committee has placed caffeine on the list of prohibited substances.

•

A $20 bill has a life span of two years.

•

The American colonies actually declared their independence from the British Empire on July 2, 1776. However, as it had only two signatures, this declaration was not approved until July 4th.

•

In 16th century Denmark, cheese was often used as currency. Perhaps you had to go to a bank when you wanted a "Provo-loan."

QUICK QUIZ

The most frequently landed-on space in Monopoly is Illinois Avenue. What's second?

Go.

Llamas usually give birth during daylight hours.

•

Nathaniel Hawthorne, Louis Armstrong, George Steinbrenner, Neil Simon and Eva Marie Saint were all born on the Fourth of July.

•

A blue whale can take in up to 10,000 gallons of water in a single feeding gulp.

•

Before St. Paul, Minnesota, became the state capital, it was named "Pig's Eye."

•

Edward Craven Walker invented the Lava Lamp in 1963.

•

A University of Washington study reported that natural redheads are more susceptible to pain.

•

The names of the signers of the *Declaration of Independence* were kept secret until 1777 in case the Revolution didn't work out. Even so, five of the men who did sign were caught and tortured by the British.

•

Albert Einstein's favorite pastime was sailing.

THOUGHTS OF THE THRONE

For her 40th birthday Sophia Loren's husband presented her with a 14-carat gold toilet seat.

There are over 11,000 species of ants.

•

Former President John Tyler joined the Confederacy and thus became the only Chief Executive ever to become a sworn enemy of the United States.

•

Frank Lloyd Wright, the famous architect, also had a hand in designing one of the biggest movie stars of the fifties. Ann Baxter is his granddaughter.

•

Three different numbers give the same result when added together as when multiplied. You know what they are, don't you? It's as easy as 1, 2, 3.

•

If you like to engage in many sesquipedalianisms, you like to use big words.

•

Elvis was once appointed Special Agent of the Bureau of Narcotics and Dangerous Drugs.

•

Elvis had a pet monkey named Scatter.

GRAFFITI

FENCING MOTTO- IN GOD WE THRUST.

It wasn't until the Civil War that specific left and right shoes were made.

•

National Park Services policy prohibits acts of violence or death scenes to be filmed in front of Mount Rushmore.

•

The inventors of Pepsi, Coke and Dr Pepper were all Civil War veterans.

•

The Indian on the Indian head penny was not an Indian at all. The model was a relative of one of the mint's officials.

•

The top lottery prizes in the world come from Spain's El Gordo-The Fat One. Players can win in excess of $300 million.

•

Adolf Hitler was a vegetarian.

•

"Mind Your Business" was the motto printed on one of the first U.S. coins.

•

George Burns was born Nathan Birnbaum.

GRAFFITI

THINK TWICE ABOUT BIGAMY:
PENALTY - TWO MOTHERS-IN-LAW.

Before getting into politics, Fidel Castro was a movie extra in Hollywood and made a film with Esther Williams.

•

Robert Todd Lincoln was present at three presidential assassinations- his father's, President Garfield's and President McKinley's.

•

Children under age 4 and adults over 50 rarely blush.

•

Kleenex tissues were first used as a filter in gas masks during World War I.

•

At the outbreak of WWI, the American Air Force consisted of only 50 men. Of course that wasn't so bad considering they only had one plane!

•

Hot Foot Teddy was Smokey Bear's original name.

•

In 1952, Queen Elizabeth was named *Time* magazine's "Man of the Year."

•

The ten most popular cat names, in order, are: Kitty, Smokey, Shadow, Tiger, Boo, Boots, Molly, Tigger, Spike and Princess.

QUICK QUIZ

Do you know the only number that is twice the sum of its digits?

18.

The longest recorded life span of a cat is 34 years.

•

Red vs. white stripes on the U.S. flag? Reds win, 7-6.

•

In Memphis, Tennessee, it's against the law for frogs to croak after 11 P.M.

•

The most married man in the monogamous world was a former Baptist minister, Glynn "Scotty" Wolfe of California, who had 27 wives.

•

It's illegal to ride a bike into a swimming pool in Baldwin Park, California.

•

The blood of a spider is transparent.

•

In 2012, London will become the first city to host the modern Olympic games three times, having previously done so in 1908 and 1948.

•

As many as 100 pearls have been found in a single oyster.

THOUGHTS OF THE THRONE

The White House has 132 rooms, including 16 family-guest rooms, 1 main kitchen, 1 diet kitchen, 1 family kitchen, and- most importantly, 35 bathrooms.

Most of the germs that get into your body enter through your mouth.

•

The original name for the portrait *Whistler's Mother* was *Arrangement in Grey and Black*.

•

DaVinci's masterpiece, *Mona Lisa*, took ten years to complete.

•

The best-selling art poster in America is van Gogh's *Starry Night*.

•

Charles Lindbergh was not the first person to cross the Atlantic in an airplane. Sixty-six people made the trip before he did. He was the first to fly alone.

•

A man with more than one wife is a polygamist. A woman with more than one husband is a polyandrist.

•

Less than half of the single men in the U.S. who've reached the age of 35 ever get married.

•

The shark in the movie *Jaws* was nicknamed Bruce.

— GRAFFITI —

HOW CAN THERE BE SELF-HELP GROUPS?

The ice covering the Arctic Ocean is 7 to 10 feet thick.

•

The Far Side's Gary Larson once ran over a dog on his way to a job interview with the Seattle Humane Society. He got the job and became an animal abuse investigator.

•

The only country whose national flag is a single color is Libya. It's green.

•

The elephant is the only animal that can't jump and the only animal with four knees.

•

Jerry Seinfeld sold light bulbs by telephone.

•

Gone with the Wind was Margaret Mitchell's only novel.

•

Calvin Coolidge was the only U.S. President born on a national holiday, July 4, 1872.

•

A survey among florists revealed that men tend to buy red flowers more than any other color.

GRAFFITI

GEORGE WASHINGTON DIDN'T BLAME
THE PREVIOUS ADMINISTRATION.

The microwave oven is used more for reheating coffee than for any other reason.

•

The one-millionth trademark from the U.S. Patent Office was granted to Sweet 'N Low.

•

The average American eats more lettuce than any other vegetable, an average of 27.4 pounds per year.

•

Mickey Mouse's nephews are Morty and Ferdy.

•

The original voice of Mickey Mouse was Walt Disney.

•

Mussolini's favorite cartoon character was Donald Duck.

•

George Washington gave New York the nickname the "Empire State".

•

A hockey rink is 200 feet long.

•

"Jack" is the most common name in nursery rhymes.

QUICK QUIZ

FACT or FIB? The Olympic flame was conceived for the Games by none other than Adolf Hitler.

FACT.

Super Bowl Sunday is the second-largest U.S. food consumption day, following Thanksgiving.

•

Employees at Disney World were not allowed to wear mustaches up until 2000.

•

Jack Nicholson single-handedly rescued five drowning people from the New Jersey surf back in the fifties.

•

The longest named phobia we came across was macroxenoglosso-phobia – a fear of long words!

•

The first drive-in theater opened in 1932 in Camden, New Jersey.

•

Cacophobia is a fear of ugliness.

•

Bibliophobia is a fear of books.

•

A Virginia law requires all bathtubs be kept in the yard and not in the house.

•

Albert Einstein never wore socks.

THOUGHTS OF THE THRONE

Before the 1986 Super Bowl, NBC gave viewers a blank screen to enable them to go to the bathroom.

Washington, D.C. has the highest ration of lawyers per resident- 1 for every 19 people.

•

It's against the law for a woman to dress as Santa in Minnesota.

•

During a single storm, the Empire State Building may be struck by lightning twenty times.

•

Rin Tin Tin and Lassie have prints on the Hollywood Walk of Fame.

•

Eleven dogs played "Lassie" in the movie and TV series. Only one was female.

•

The only animal to be awarded both the Purple Heart and Silver Star during World War II was Chips, a K-9 dog.

•

"You dirty rat" is a line attributed to James Cagney, but never used by him in any movie.

•

Roy Rogers is the only person ever elected to the Country Music Hall of Fame twice.

GRAFFITI

IT'S NOT WHETHER YOU WIN OR LOSE –
UNTIL YOU LOSE.

In his last will, after disposition of an estate of $65,000, Einstein left his manuscripts to Hebrew University and his violin to his grandson.

•

Rocky Lane, a cowboy film actor, was the voice of that talking horse, Mr. Ed.

•

The only fruit to have its seeds on the outside is the strawberry.

•

Albert Einstein was offered the presidency of Israel in 1952 but turned it down.

•

James Madison was the first President to wear long pants; his predecessors all wore knickers.

•

Pink lemonade was created in 1857 by Pete Conklin, who unwittingly used a bucket of water in which a circus performer had soaked his red tights.

•

The most common name for a town in the United States is Fairview.

•

When asked to name a color, the most common answer is "red".

── GRAFFITI ──────────────────

WHAT HAPPENED TO THE FIRST 6 "UPS"?

The first newspaper crossword puzzle, by Arthur Wynne, appeared in the *New York World* on December 21, 1913.

·

More than half of the cucumbers grown in the U.S. are for pickles.

·

The most common last name initial in the United States is "S."

·

The first supermarket was established in 1916 when Clarence Saunders set up shop with the Piggley Wiggley self-service food mart in Memphis, Tennessee.

·

Gene Conley is the only athlete to play on world championship teams in both Major League Baseball and in pro basketball.

·

Transsexual Renee Richards (nee Richard Raskind) is the only tennis player to compete in both the men's and women's singles at the U.S. Open.

·

Henry David Thoreau's last words, uttered on May 6, 1862, were "Moose, Indian." Their meaning is unknown.

·

Lewis Carroll wrote *Alice's Adventures in Wonderland* standing up.

QUICK QUIZ

How many holes are there in a standard wiffle ball?

8.

T. S. Eliot's initials stand for Thomas Stearns.

•

Four out of five people who try out a new pen will write their own name.

•

40 out of 100 Americans eat cereal for breakfast every day.

•

Spencer Tracy was once given an Academy Award engraved to "Dick Tracy".

•

Ventriloquist Edgar Bergen (and his dummy, Charlie McCarthy) received the only wooden Oscar.

•

President Barack Obama is left-handed and so were three of the last four chief executives- Bill Clinton, George H.W. Bush and Ronald Reagan (who was ambidextrous). Only George W. Bush was right-handed.

•

A clothes designer in New Jersey once designed a jacket with 89 zippers.

•

If the coils of the French horn were straightened out, the instrument would be 22 feet long.

Thoughts of the Throne

The most difficult common item to flush is a ping-pong ball.
(WARNING: not responsible for any plumbing bills
incurred because you decided to double-check us.)

The White House is the most visited home in the United States. Second is Graceland, the former home of Elvis Presley, in Memphis, Tennessee.

•

Fairy tale writer Hans Christian Anderson was dyslexic. Others afflicted by dyslexia include Thomas Edison, Woodrow Wilson, Tom Cruise and Henry Winkler.

•

Three out of four Americans like to doodle.

•

Aesop was believed to have been a dwarf.

•

An ostrich can cover 25 feet in a single stride.

•

Most hummingbirds weigh less than a penny.

•

To bankers, ZIP is an acronym for Zero Interest Payment.

•

To psychologists, ZIP is short for Zero Intelligence Potential.

•

To postal workers, ZIP stands for Zoning Improvement Plan.

— GRAFFITI —

SQUARE BATHTUBS DON'T HAVE RINGS.

A butterfly flaps its wings about 300 times a minute.

•

A penguin is the only bird that can swim but not fly.

•

The largest flying bird is the albatross.

•

The Vice-President lives at Number One Observatory Circle, on the grounds of the United States Naval Observatory in Washington, D.C.

•

In *I Love Lucy,* the Ricardos lived at 623 East 68th Street in Manhattan.

•

1 Cherry Street in New York City was home to George Washington. It was the first U.S. presidential address.

•

There are 575 words in the epic poem *Casey at the Bat.*

•

Rocker Rod Stewart was once a gravedigger.

•

Entertainer Victor Borge used to play the organ at funerals.

GRAFFITI

CANARY CAUGHT IN LAWN MOWER
IS SHREDDED TWEET.

The bite of a cobra is deadly enough to kill even an elephant if it's bitten on the trunk tip or the base of the toenail.

•

Tombstones were originally placed on plots over the dead so that the deceased could not come out and harm the living.

•

Alfred Blozis set the world record for the hand grenade toss back in 1944 when he lobbed the old pineapple 284 1/2 feet.

•

There is a tribe of athletes in Burma called the Intha that row their longboats with their legs.

•

The award presented to *Sports Illustrated* magazine's Sportsman of the Year is a Grecian urn.

•

The inscription on actress Joan Hackett's grave marker reads, "Go Away! I'm Sleeping."

•

The phrase "stone broke" comes from the Middle Age custom of breaking stone benches of craftsmen who were unable to pay their debts.

QUICK QUIZ

What two fifteen-letter words are spelled exactly the same except for the first letter?

Rationalization and nationalization.

37% of Americans own dogs, 26% have cats in their household, and 5% have birds.

•

When the mood of an octopus changes, so does its color.

•

A cow spends approximately 18 out of every 24 hours chewing on something.

•

The leader of a wolf pack is always female.

•

When J.C. Penney opened his first store in Ohio in 1902, it was called The Golden Rule.

•

J.C. Penney's middle name was Cash.

•

Sam Walton's first job was at J.C. Penney.

•

There are more words in the English language than any other language in the world.

•

Johann Sebastian Bach fathered 20 children.

THOUGHTS OF THE THRONE

*Until 1978, a Connecticut law required
that all toilets have horseshoe-shaped seats.*

Bookkeeper is the only word in the English language that has three consecutive sets of double letters.

•

There are 20 possible opening moves in chess.

•

Bill Cullen holds the record for hosting the most TV game shows – 20.

•

Lampoon is a French phrase meaning "Let's drink!"

•

Robot comes from the Czech word for Slave.

•

P.T. Barnum coined the phrase "Siamese twins."

•

Carl Stotz invented Little League baseball.

•

Joey Jay was the first Little Leaguer to play in the big leagues.

•

A died-in-the-wool Democrat, Harry Truman refused to have anything to do with Dumbo the Elephant in a 1957 visit to Disneyland.

GRAFFITI

IS THERE ANOTHER WORD FOR SYNONYM?

Nine-tenths of the ice in the world can be found in Antarctica.

•

If you discount the "North" and "South" in the Americas, each of the world's continents begin and end with the same letter (e.g., EuropE, AmericA, AsiA).

•

The white shark has a perpetual appetite. No matter how much it eats, it is always hungry.

•

A jellyfish that has been dead for months can still sting you if you walk on it in bare feet.

•

The jawbone is the hardest bone in the body.

•

Harvey Ball drew the first Smiley Face in 1963.

•

A golf ball cannot weigh more than 1.62 ounces or be smaller than 1.68 inches in diameter.

•

Bowling pins are made out of maple.

•

One out of ten Americans reads the Bible every day.

GRAFFITI

BUTCHERS MAKE BOTH ENDS MEAT.

Ben Franklin coined the phrase, "An apple a day keeps the doctor away."

•

Sister Mary Carolyn was elected mayor of Dubuque, Iowa, in 1980, the only nun to ever hold that office in an American city.

•

Harry Potter author J.K. Rowling is the first person to become a billionaire by writing books.

•

There are no clocks in gambling casinos.

•

President Roosevelt nicknamed his political advisors the "Tennis Cabinet."

•

The President and Vice-President of the United States are not allowed to travel together.

•

Candice Bergen of *Boston Legal* was once offered a spot on *60 Minutes*.

•

Early watches had only one hand that indicated the hour.

QUICK QUIZ

Where's the only place that the American flag flies all day, never goes up, comes down, nor flies at half-mast?

The moon.

Bono's real name is Paul Hewson.

•

Josephine Esther Mentzer underwent a cosmetic name change to Estee Lauder.

•

Clay Aiken was born Clayton Holmes Grissom.

•

It takes about a yard of sugar cane to make one sugar cube.

•

It took a 1893 Supreme Court ruling to declare the tomato a vegetable rather than a fruit.

•

In 1915 the average annual American family income was $687.

•

17% of Americans move each year.

•

2 out of 3 people can name the three Rice Krispies characters.

•

100 million Americans drink three cups of coffee daily.

•

Rice is eaten by one half of all the people in the world every day.

THOUGHTS OF THE THRONE

When the Hoberg Paper Company people first made their soft toilet tissue in 1928, one of their employees said it was "charming." The company decided to leave the g off charming, change the pronunciation, and there you have it – simply Charmin.

Deviled eggs are so-called because when they were first made, they were covered with such hot pepper that it supposedly reminded one of the fires of hell.

•

The higher a plane flies, the less fuel it uses as the atmosphere is thinner and the vehicle meets less resistance.

•

The wingspan of a Boeing 747 is greater than the entire flying distance of the Wright Brothers' famous first foray into the wild blue yonder.

•

Just in case you weren't sure- of the Wright brothers, it was Orville who made the first airplane flight, at 10:35 a.m. on December 17, 1903.

•

King Camp Gillette created the safety razor with throwaway blades in 1895.

•

The electric razor was invented by Jacob Schick in 1928.

•

The average man spends about 3,500 hours shaving in his lifetime.

GRAFFITI

A DEAD FLOWER IS A LATE BLOOMER.

Cold-blooded animals do not dream.

•

Reindeer are superb swimmers.

•

In 1993 Ireland's Eamonn Coghlan ran the mile in 3 minutes, 58.15 seconds, becoming the first man over 40 to run a mile in less than four minutes.

•

A jogger's heel strikes the ground 1,500 times a mile.

•

In the United States a car is stolen every thirty seconds.

•

The busiest phone number in New York City is 911, with about 18,000 calls pouring in per day.

•

A rat can go longer without water than a camel.

•

Rats can't vomit.

•

Last Chance Gulch, the 1860s mining camp, later changed its name to Helena and is now the capital of Montana.

GRAFFITI

SHOULDN'T IT BE FORTH AND BACK?

Quick - which travels farther on a bike, the front wheel or back wheel? It's the front wheel, which moves back and forth as the bike is steered while the back wheel travels in a straight path.

•

Your skin weighs twice as much as your brain.

•

The human tooth has approximately fifty miles of canals in it.

•

Your heel is the body part least sensitive to pain.

•

Christmas is celebrated with fireworks in Brazil.

•

Caves have been found in every state except Rhode Island.

•

It would take twenty states the size of New Hampshire to fill up the state of Texas.

•

Florida's state song is *Old Folks at Home.*

•

IBM was originally called the Computing-Tabulating-Recording Company.

QUICK QUIZ

What's the most popular first name for a U.S. President?

James – There were six–Madison, Monroe, Polk, Buchanan, Garfield, and Carter.

The Gap clothing store chain opened in 1969 in San Francisco and was named by its owners, Donald and Doris Fisher, after the "generation gap".

•

Nike was initially named Blue Ribbon Sports. The athletic shoe-makers changed the name in 1968 to Nike after the Greek goddess of victory.

•

The Washington Monument sinks an average of six inches a year.

•

The presidential mansion in South Korea is known as the Blue House.

•

The New Orleans Hornets of the NBA are the only professional sports team with an insect's name.

•

The Utah Jazz name stems from when they played in New Orleans.

•

The Los Angeles Lakers name comes from Minnesota, the "Land of a Thousand Lakes," where they originally played.

•

A tuna can swim a hundred miles in one day.

THOUGHTS OF THE THRONE

A place called City of Rocks, New Mexico, is home to Toilet Rock, a natural rock formation shaped like a flush toilet.

Approximately 98% of all coupons go unused.

•

A hippopotamus can outrun a man.

•

It takes a skunk three weeks to crank out one ounce of foul odor.

•

Silly statute: You can be fined for playing dominoes in Alabama on Sunday.

•

It is illegal to hunt camels in Arizona.

•

Every citizen of Kentucky is required by law to take a bath once a year.

•

Birds are even more warm-blooded than mammals. A body temperature of 108 degrees is not uncommon.

•

Emperor penguins have square pupils.

•

Speaking of eyesight, you can forget about the color red, as in cape, being a factor in bullfights. Bulls are colorblind.

GRAFFITI

HEALTH FOOD IS SICKENING.

The city of Los Angeles employs a professional skunk hunter.

•

Black sheep have a keener sense of smell than white sheep.

•

Canines with the best eyesight? Greyhounds rule.

•

People magazine selected Norma Jean Baker as the Sexiest Woman of the 20th Century. You know her better as Marilyn Monroe.

•

In the wintertime squirrels lose about half of their nuts because they forget where they stored them.

•

Meteorologically speaking, partly cloudy and partly sunny means the same thing.

•

Canada has more lakes than the rest of the world put together.

•

CHOICE COD – Hold this upside-down in front of a mirror and you'll see that the first two words of this item read the same.

•

The average person's bones weigh forty pounds.

GRAFFITI

STUCCO –
WHAT YOU GET WHEN YOU SIT ON GUMMO.

The Sahara Desert is expanding south at the rate of about a half-mile a year.

•

An adult's hair can stretch 25% of its length without breaking.

•

According to Harper's Index, 80% of Americans believe in miracles.

•

Frank Lloyd Wright wore elevator shoes.

•

The odds of flipping a coin heads up ten times in a row are 1,023 to 1.

•

Tycoon J. Paul Getty was once a sparring partner for heavyweight champion Jack Dempsey.

•

Tug-of-war began as a sport in ancient China.

•

At Four Corners you can walk in Utah, Colorado, Arizona and New Mexico within seconds.

QUICK QUIZ

Name the original hosts of *Jeopardy!, Hollywood Squares,* and *Who Wants to be a Millionaire?*

Art Fleming, Peter Marshall, and Regis Philbin, respectively.

There has been only one Triple Crown winner that sired another Triple Crown winner. Gallant Fox was the father, Omaha the offspring.

•

George Jung, a Los Angeles noodlemaker, invented fortune cookies in 1916.

•

Louis Pasteur was so obsessive about germs that he refused to shake hands with people.

•

In the Philippine jungles the yo-yo was first used as a weapon.

•

Donald Duck's nephews, Huey, Dewey and Louie, have no father.

•

Ruth G. Wakefield invented the chocolate chip cookie in 1930.

•

Caesar salad has nothing to do with the rulers of Rome. It was first made in a Tijuana bar in the twenties.

•

The second most popular Father's Day gift is shaving lotion. We think you know what's first.

THOUGHTS OF THE THRONE

Actress Susan Sarandon proudly displays her Oscars and other awards in the bathroom.

The average American has a 10,000 word vocabulary.

•

A snake can hear with its tongue.

•

During the Korean War, baseball's Cincinnati Reds changed their name to the Redlegs for political reasons.

•

The "Hollywood" sign in California was originally "Hollywood-land" but the last four letters fell down during World War II.

•

Trumpeter Herb Alpert played taps for military funerals.

•

George H.W. Bush, at eighteen, was the youngest Navy pilot of WWII.

•

Football historians claim the quarterback's exclamation of "hut" for the snap stems from Army drills where the drill sergeant would count off "Hut-2-3-4."

•

Winnie-the-Pooh creator A. A. Milne's initials stand for Alan Alexander.

GRAFFITI

MAN WHO WANTS PRETTY
NURSE MUST BE PATIENT.

Casanova was a novel lover who ended his life as a librarian.

•

The first live televised murder occurred in 1963, when Jack Ruby killed JFK's assassin, Lee Harvey Oswald.

•

A 93-year-old Australian man, Les Colley, became the oldest father ever when his wife gave birth to a son, Oswald, in 1992.

•

John Greenwood was the dentist who made George Washington's false teeth.

•

The Alaskan flag was designed by a thirteen-year-old student who won an American Legion contest.

•

The longest place name in the United States is also the longest name of a lake in the world –
Lake Chargogagogmanchaugagogchaubunagamaug.

•

A prairie dog isn't a dog. It's a rodent.

•

Dave Thomas, the founder of Wendy's, named the fast food restaurant after his daughter.

GRAFFITI

DO LIPTON TEA EMPLOYEES
TAKE COFFEE BREAKS?

The Red Sea is not red. It's bluish-green.

•

Ida May Fuller of Vermont was the first person to receive a Social Security check. She got it in 1940 and lived to be over 100, eventually collecting more than $20,000.

•

In 1950 the town of Hot Springs, New Mexico, renamed itself Truth or Consequences in honor of the game show.

•

The numbers in a single Sudoku puzzle add up to 405.

•

The newspaper in Popeye's hometown of Sweethaven is called the *Sweethaven Daily Poop*.

•

Howdy Doody's sister was named Heidi Doody.

•

On June 19, 1989, "Bud" was the first tropical storm to be named after a male.

•

The average winter temperature in Iceland is warmer than in Chicago.

QUICK QUIZ

Mildred and Patty Hill are in the musical history books for what reason?

They wrote *Happy Birthday to You.*

Liberace started out by giving concerts at high schools under the name of Walter Busterkeys.

•

The last act at Woodstock was Jimi Hendrix.

•

The national anthem of China is *March On, March On.*

•

Goldie was Smokey Bear's mate. She bore him Smokey Bear II.

•

The only dog that sweats is the Mexican hairless.

•

The early bird may catch the worm but the poorwill catches a snooze. It is the only bird that hibernates.

•

Weatherman Willard Scott was the original Ronald McDonald.

•

The most popular hobby in the world is stamp collecting.

•

Eat a raw cashew and you may "cash-ew" in your chips. A cashew contains poisonous oil and needs to be roasted before it is safe for eating.

THOUGHTS OF THE THRONE

An all-important statistical survey found that 88% of Americans say they'd replace an empty roll of toilet tissue rather than leave the chore to the next person.

Cajun chef Paul Prudhomme weighed 500 pounds at the age of fifteen.

•

The twin Popsicle was created during the Depression so that two children could share a single treat.

•

According to the *New England Journal of Medicine*, if your left thumbnail is wider and squarer at the base than the right one, you're a southpaw (and vice-versa).

•

Dogs can understand about a two hundred word human vocabulary while a cat comprehends only about fifty words.

•

Big Bird from *Sesame Street* has a teddy bear named Radar.

•

The original working title of The Beatles' hit song *Yesterday* was *Scrambled Eggs*.

•

About the $24 Peter Minuet paid to the American Indians for Manhattan- invested at 8% compounded daily, that money would be worth more than 30 trillion dollars today.

GRAFFITI

HE WHO STICK HEAD IN OPEN WINDOW
GET PANE IN NECK.

Paul Newman, Hugh Downs and Jack Nicklaus are colorblind.

•

Jackie Gleason wrote the theme song for *The Honeymooners*.

•

An ant's sense of smell is just as good as a dog's.

•

Chuck Berry had but a single number one hit, *My Ding-a-Ling*, in 1972.

•

In Tiddlywinks the art of flipping the winks into a cup is called "Potting".

•

According to Guinness the world's hardest tongue twister is this: "The sixth sick sheik's sixth sheep's sick."

•

The President of the United States receives more than 20,000 letters in the mail every day.

•

"Double hemisphere action" is the term used for the ability to write, simultaneously, something completely different with both your left and right hands.

GRAFFITI

A SENTENCE IS A GOOD THING TO PUT A PREPOSITION AT THE END OF.

Red schoolhouses were painted red for an elementary reason – it was the cheapest color.

•

Retlaw Yensid was the writer of the 1966 Disney movie *Lt. Robin Crusoe, U.S.N.* Retlaw Yensid is Walter Disney backwards.

•

"Chop suey" means "odds and ends."

•

The color red is not generally used in the packaging of ice cream because it reminds people of heat.

•

The 1,500 pound leatherback turtle carries a shell that is as big as a king size bed, but a lot harder to find fitted sheets for.

•

An elephant smells through its mouth, not its trunk.

•

The most common albino animal is the Siamese cat.

•

Abraham Lincoln was a licensed bartender.

•

A numerym is a word for a phone number that spells a word.

QUICK QUIZ

Who was the very first host of *Saturday Night Live?*

George Carlin, on October 11, 1975.

The average magazine lies around the house for 29 weeks before someone gets around to throwing it out.

•

Half the world's lemons grow in the United States, mostly in California.

•

An avocado has 370 calories, the greatest number of any fruit.

•

Pineapples are not native to Hawaii. They were first planted there in 1790.

•

An excerpt from the diary of King George III of England stated, "Nothing of importance happened today." It was dated 7/4/1776.

•

Calvin Coolidge was the only President to have been sworn in by his own father.

•

Coolidge loved to fish, but always wore gloves and made sure the Secret Service men handled the worms.

•

Thomas Edison was 32 when he invented the light bulb.

THOUGHTS OF THE THRONE

About one third of people flush
while they are still sitting on the toilet.

The wood used to make Lincoln Logs comes from the forests of Oregon.

•

Harry S Truman's first full day as President was on a Friday the 13th.

•

When Oreo cookies were first made, they were mound-shaped. The name comes from the Greek word "oreo" which means "hill."

•

1812 Overture composer Tchaikovsky suffered from nervous disorders, hallucinations and a morbid fear that his head would roll off his shoulders while conducting the orchestra.

•

The Lone Ranger's sidekick was Tonto, who was played by Jay Silverheels who was born Harold J. Smith.

•

Peter Graves is the younger brother of James Arness.

•

Before making a name for herself as an opera star, Beverly Sills was known as Belle "Bubbles" Silverman.

•

Elephants can get flat feet.

GRAFFITI

TWO WRONGS MAY NOT MAKE RIGHT;
BUT TWO WRIGHTS MAKE AIRPLANE.

The Rolls Royce Corporation was founded in 1904 by two Englishmen, Charles Stewart Rolls and Sir Frederick Henry Royce.

•

The largest production car ever made was the 1927 Golden Bugatti. It measured 27 feet from bumper to bumper. Only six of these were ever made and some are still around.

•

The first person to be arrested for speeding was a New York City cab driver. On May 20, 1899, Jacob German was arrested for doing a breakneck 12 mph.

•

Avon, the cosmetics giant, got its name because the founder was fond of Shakespeare, so the company was named after Stratford-on-Avon.

•

The K in K-Mart stands for Kresge, from Sebastian S. Kresge, who founded the store in Detroit in 1897.

•

Ketchup was originally a Chinese medicine.

•

2.8 million pieces of airline luggage are misrouted every year.

GRAFFITI

WHEN CHEESE GETS ITS PICTURE TAKEN, WHAT DOES IT SAY?

The average American laughs fifteen times a day.

•

Your nose and ears never stop growing.

•

Dr. Seuss coined the term "nerd".

•

Greer Garson delivered the longest acceptance speech ever in the history of the Academy Awards when she won the Oscar for Best Actress in *Mrs. Miniver*. Her speech lasted thirty minutes.

•

Edgar Allan Poe often wrote his works with his cat seated on his shoulder.

•

Dogs are more likely to have a nervous breakdown than any other non-human animal.

•

Each of your toes has three bones except for your big toe, which has but two.

•

The first female cabinet member was Frances Perkins, appointed by FDR in 1933 as Secretary of Labor.

QUICK QUIZ

The letter "j" appears in the name of how many states in the U.S.?

Just 1 – New Jersey.

U.S. paper currency measures 6 1/8 by 2 9/16 inches.

•

A group of swans is called a bevy.

•

Gerald Ford was the only American President to have been a male model. He modeled winter sports clothes for *Look* magazine in 1939.

•

In baseball, a ball that landed in fair territory and bounced into the stands was counted as a home run until 1931.

•

Softball was originally called "kitten ball."

•

The oldest bridegroom in history was Ralph Cambridge, who was 105 when he tied the knot with his 70-year-old bride, Adriana Kapp.

•

Turn-of-the-20th-century multimillionaire Russell Sage amassed much of his money by never buying underwear. You could say he saved all his long john silver!

•

The word "karate" means "empty hand."

THOUGHTS OF THE THRONE

A poll conducted by The Scott Paper Company reveals that, by a four-to-one margin, people ages 50 and over prefer to have their toilet paper dispensed over-the-top.

Lady Randolph Churchill, Winston's mother, invented the Manhattan cocktail in 1874.

•

The official state sport of Maryland is jousting.

•

Sleepwalking is hereditary- and 2.5% of Americans do it regularly.

•

Dorothy's pet cow in *The Wizard of Oz* was named Imogene.

•

Great Danes come from Germany, not Denmark.

•

Albert Einstein's brain is in a mason jar in a Wichita, Kansas, laboratory.

•

In the 19th century, nine pins were used in bowling.

•

U.S. Presidents U.S. Grant, William Howard Taft, Herbert Hoover and Dwight D. Eisenhower never held any other elective office.

•

The oldest subway in the world went into service in 1863 in London.

GRAFFITI

MAN WHO LEAP OFF CLIFF
JUMP TO CONCLUSION.

If you think you eat like a bird, think again. Birds eat from one quarter to one half their body weight every day.

•

Alligator shirts have crocodiles on them.

•

The Roman Coliseum was formerly called the Flavian Amphitheater.

•

Al Capone carried a business card stating that he was "a second hand furniture dealer."

•

Henry Wadsworth Longfellow is the only American whose bust is in Westminster Abbey.

•

It doesn't matter what the birth certificate says in England; all royal birthdays are celebrated in June.

•

The largest fruit crop on earth is grapes.

•

Ernest Hemingway rewrote the last page of *A Farewell to Arms* 39 times.

GRAFFITI

MARRIAGE IS THE CHIEF REASON
FOR DIVORCE.

In the James Bond novels by Ian Fleming, the Bond family's motto was "The World is Not Enough."

•

The average garden variety caterpillar has 228 muscles in its head.

•

Horatio Alger wrote 119 full-length novels in 30 years.

•

Frank Lloyd Wright coined the word "carport".

•

In 1938 Charles Zibbleman swam the Hudson River from Albany to New York City, traveling 147 miles and setting the record for handicapped swimmers. Zibbleman had no legs.

•

A pro golfer whacks the ball at 170 mph or more.

•

The delicious apple was originally called the Hawkeye.

•

The average American eats 1,889 Tootsie Rolls in a lifetime.

•

Do you sleep in your birthday suit? 20% of men and 6% of women say they do.

QUICK QUIZ

What's the only word in the English language
that begins and ends with "und"?

Underground.

A watermelon is 92% water.

•

Van Gogh signed his paintings with his first name, Vincent.

•

Life Savers are the best-selling candy in the world.

•

Sir Walter Raleigh is buried with his favorite pipe and a tin of tobacco.

•

Statistics show that Saturday is the most dangerous day to drive an automobile.

•

Except for the Bible, Benjamin Spock's *Common Sense Book of Baby and Child Care* is the best selling non-fiction book of all time.

•

The Mason-Dixon Line was named for the surveyors Charles Mason and Jeremiah Dixon.

•

Leonardo da Vinci had trouble finishing anything. His interest would always wander to something else and he left a trail of partially completed works across Italy.

THOUGHTS OF THE THRONE

According to the *San Diego Union,* the odds are 1 out of 10,000 (.001%) that you'll suffer a toilet-related injury this year.

The Pieta was the only one of Michelangelo's sculptures that he signed.

•

Alaska is almost three times the size of Texas.

•

The Rolling Stones got their name from *Rolling Stone Blues* by Muddy Waters.

•

There are 66 acceptable two-letter words in Scrabble.

•

When you breathe, the speed of your exhaled air is about 15 miles per hour.

•

Seven letters in the English alphabet can double as Roman numerals- I, L, V, D, X, C, and M.

•

It was (and maybe still is) illegal to wear roller skates in a Portland, Oregon, restroom.

•

James Whistler had to buy back his most famous painting, *Whistler's Mother*, from a pawnshop after his mother passed away.

GRAFFITI

ON WALL STREET,
EVERY BULL HAS A BEAR BEHIND.

Arizona had a statute making it illegal to hunt camels in that state.

•

In New York it is illegal to shoot at a rabbit from a moving trolley car.

•

Each quill of the porcupine has about 1,000 tiny sharp barbs.

•

A full-grown circus lion consumes about 30 pounds of horsemeat a day.

•

A pig always sleeps on its right side.

•

President George W. Bush met Laura at a backyard barbecue.

•

Henry Ford invented charcoal briquettes.

•

Yes, there is a Hamburger Hall of Fame, and it's located in Seymour, Wisconsin.

•

The largest single edition of *The New York Times*, dated Sunday, October 10, 1971, had fifteen sections with a total of 972 pages. Each copy weighed over seven pounds.

GRAFFITI

IF AT FIRST YOU DON'T SUCCEED,
THAT'S IT FOR SKYDIVING.

Over one million drawings went into the movie production of *Pinocchio*.

•

The *New York Herald* was the newspaper employer of Oscar Madison on the TV sitcom *The Odd Couple*.

•

The country of Paraguay doesn't use coins, just paper money.

•

Portland is the largest city in two different states.

•

Manhole covers are made round because they can't fall through the manhole itself. Other shapes can.

•

Former astronaut John Glenn and baseball great Ted Williams were co-pilots during Korean War bombing missions.

•

A stack of a trillion new one-dollar bills would reach 69,000 miles high.

•

The life span of a baseball in a major league game is seven pitches.

QUICK QUIZ

How old was Elvis when he died?

42.

If you take a penny and double it, and then keep doubling it every day for thirty days, you will wind up with over five million dollars.

•

Mordecai Brown, one of the greatest pitchers in the history of baseball, had only three fingers on his pitching hand.

•

A female rabbit is called a doe; a male is a buck.

•

A violin contains seventy separate pieces of wood.

•

Roller skates, which originally consisted of four wheels on rubber pads, were invented around 1860.

•

Studies show that Americans favor pepperoni more than any other pizza topping.

•

When Henry VIII became the King of England in 1509, he was only 17 years old.

•

Smithsonian Institution founder James Smith never set foot in the United States.

THOUGHTS OF THE THRONE

Circle your calendar – World Toilet Day is November 19th. Maybe they should just call it "Tanksgiving."

Writers Art Buchwald and Harold Robbins, both orphans, were raised in various foster homes.

•

Bowling pins are 12" apart.

•

"Dare to Be Free" was the slogan of the American Revolution.

•

Yankee Doodle was composed in England as an anti-American tune.

•

The Union Army lost more men to disease than battle during the Civil War.

•

Herbert Hoover was the first President to have a phone on his desk.

•

According to the latest census, there are 4.1 million American natives in the U.S.

•

Back in Pilgrim days, a woman who reached the age of thirty and was unmarried was called a thornback.

GRAFFITI

HOW DO YOU KNOW WHEN YOU
RUN OUT OF INVISIBLE INK?

Mary Phelps Jacobs patented the first brassiere in November of 1914.

•

In 1901 Annie Taylor was the first woman to go over Niagara Falls in a barrel and survive.

•

A 1973 Macon, Georgia, minor league hockey team was named the Macon "Whoopies" after the song *Makin' Whoopie.*

•

Chop Suey originated in California.

•

Thomas Edison was hard of hearing and often communicated with his wife in Morse code.

•

In Japan, the most common name to see in the phone book is Minoru Suzukis.

•

Lemonade is the top-selling Kool-Aid flavor.

•

If you're the typical American man, you own 22 ties.

•

You use 72 muscles to speak one word.

GRAFFITI

TWO WRONGS NOT MAKE RIGHT,
BUT THREE LEFTS DO.

Stan Laurel was married eight times; however, he only had four wives.

•

Whoopi Goldberg's real name is Caryn Johnson.

•

Queen Elizabeth I suffered from smallpox and was completely bald by the age of 29.

•

Arlington National Cemetery was once the site of Robert E. Lee's home.

•

Scrabble and Monopoly were two of Elvis Presley's favorite games.

•

American Revolutionary War hero John Paul Jones became an admiral in the Russian Navy.

•

A woman can talk with less effort than a man because her vocal chords are shorter.

•

If you plan on being buried in a standard grave, your permanent "living" quarters will be 7'8" long x 3'2" wide and, or course, 6' deep.

QUICK QUIZ

Who was the only President in U.S. history to ever be divorced?

Ronald Reagan.

A man's beard grows about an inch in eight weeks.

•

Approximately one out of every six adult male Americans weighs more than 200 pounds.

•

Babies have over 60 more bones than adults.

•

Blood takes about 23 seconds to make one round trip of your body.

•

60% of our body weight is water.

•

About one in six people is an habitual fingernail biter.

•

There are 140 languages spoken around the world and each is spoken by more than one million people.

•

The word "amen" is spoken in more tongues than any other word.

•

Floccinaucinihilipilification is the longest nonscientific word in the dictionary. According to Webster's, it is "an act or instance of judging something to be worthless or trivial" (maybe the word itself?).

THOUGHTS OF THE THRONE

Dr. Richard Deutsch invented talking urinal cakes, which warn would-be drunk drivers that they may be over the legal limit.

Two-thirds of mankind is right-handed.

•

Over half of all Americans wind up wearing some kind of corrective lenses.

•

A mosquito has 47 teeth.

•

Mosquitoes can drink twice their weight in blood.

•

A mosquito's favorite aroma is aftershave.

•

L.L. Bean's initials stand for Leon Leonwood.

•

Richard Nixon's presidency officially ended while he was flying over Kansas City.

•

The Russian word "kremlin" means "castle".

•

A gnu has the feet of an antelope, the name and body of an ass, the head and humped shoulders of a buffalo and the beard of a goat.

GRAFFITI

A CLOSED MOUTH GATHERS NO FOOT.

Songwriter Irving Berlin could not read music and could only play the black keys on a piano.

•

Woodpeckers don't get headaches.

•

There's been only one Roman Catholic U.S. President – John F. Kennedy.

•

There are 3,070 counties in the United States.

•

Of the 3,000 islands that comprise The Bahamas chain in The Caribbean, only 20 are inhabited.

•

Pigs look like they're tiptoeing because they walk on only two of four toes on each foot.

•

Hogs eat any and all kinds of snakes.

•

Opossums do not play dead. They are actually fainting.

•

Sir Winston Churchill was the first honorary citizen of the United States.

GRAFFITI

WHAT WAS THE BEST THING
BEFORE SLICED BREAD?

All polar bears are left-handed.

•

The Campbell's Soup red and white label was inspired by the colors of the Cornell University football team.

•

Brokers Tip won only one race in its entire career- the Kentucky Derby.

•

The day after meeting Lady Bird, former President Lyndon B. Johnson proposed. They were married two months later.

•

The owl is a real bird-brain and not wise. Crows are thought to be the smartest birds.

•

The largest shopping mall in the U.S. is the Mall of America in Bloomington, Minnesota.

•

A hurricane, typhoon and cyclone are all the same thing.

•

Lee Trevino, Jerry Heard and Bobby Nichols were all struck by lightning during the same golf tournament in 1975.

QUICK QUIZ

How many sides are there on a quindecagon?

15.

Three-fourths of all pencils sold in the U.S. are yellow-painted.

•

The standard size of a credit card is 3 3/8" by 2 1/8."

•

The French poodle originated in Germany.

•

June 16, 1976, marked the first "rain-in" of a baseball game. The Houston Astros - Pittsburgh Pirates contest was called off because severe flooding made it impossible for fans to get to the Astrodome.

•

The score of a forfeited NFL game is 2-0.

•

Edgar Allan Poe was expelled from West Point in 1831 when he appeared at a parade in his birthday suit.

•

Sandhurst is the British equivalent of West Point. Ian Fleming and David Niven were graduates.

•

The first modern traffic light stopped traffic on Euclid Avenue in Cleveland in 1914.

THOUGHTS OF THE THRONE

Alaska has more outhouses than any other U.S. state.

In the U.S. a baby is born every 8 1/2 seconds.

•

When George Washington made the Marquis de Lafayette a major general in the Continental Army, the Frenchman was only 19.

•

Bubble gum first appeared in 1933, but it wasn't until 1947 that Topps Chewing Gum Company started to produce Bazooka.

According to the FDA, two out of five women dye their hair.

•

Mickey Mantle's home jersey #7 from 1960 sold for $101,410- about $40,000 more than his salary that year- at a sports memorabilia auction conducted by Lelands in Seaford, N.Y., in 2007.

•

If the wire of a Slinky was laid out flat, it would measure 87 feet.

•

The first United States medical school was established in Philadelphia in 1765.

•

You have a 1 in 600,000 chance of being struck by lightning sometime during your life.

─── GRAFFITI ───

THE METRIC SYSTEM
DOESN'T MEASURE UP.

Irving Berlin was the only person in the history of the Academy of Motion Picture Arts and Sciences ever to present an Oscar to himself.

•

All racehorses celebrate their birthdays on January 1st.

•

A shrimp's heart rules its head- probably because that's exactly where it is!

•

The most popular crossword puzzle subject is the Bible.

•

Baseball great Jackie Robinson's brother Mack finished second to Jesse Owens in the 200-meter race in the 1936 Olympics.

•

Bob Newhart's real first name is George.

•

Soap operas were so named because most of the sponsors were soap companies.

•

The letters LED on a digital watch stand for "light-emitting diode".

GRAFFITI

HOW DO THEY GET A DEER TO CROSS AT THE YELLOW ROAD SIGN?

Dr. Martin Luther King, Jr.'s first name was Michael.

•

Home plate in baseball was square until 1900, when it was made five-sided to help umpires in calling balls and strikes.

•

Liberace owned a $200,000 tea set that once belonged to Napoleon.

•

Early American colonists made gray paint for their homes by boiling blueberries in milk.

•

Wonder Bread introduced sliced bread in 1930.

•

Just how fast is a snail's pace? About 25 feet per hour for most species.

•

In 1931 Cleveland Indians catcher Joe Sprinz caught a baseball dropped 800 feet from a balloon. The impact created such a jolt through his body that he broke his jaw.

•

A soap bubble's wall is but a few millionths of an inch thick.

QUICK QUIZ

What is Paul McCartney's first name?

James.

The geographic center of the U.S. is located near Castle Rock, South Dakota.

•

Electric fans actually increase the temperature of the air.

•

One pound of nickel can be stretched into a fine wire eighty miles long.

•

Tiny earthworms have five hearts.

•

A humpback whale can travel up to 4,000 miles in a year.

•

The hippopotamus has skin two inches thick in some places.

•

A football is made of cowhide, not pigskin.

•

The most change you could have without being able to break a dollar is $1.19 (three quarters, four dimes and four pennies).

•

San Francisco has the largest Chinese population outside the Orient.

THOUGHTS OF THE THRONE

In 1840, poet Henry Wadsworth Longfellow became the first American to have plumbing installed in his house.

The highest sand dunes in the world are in the Sahara. They build up to a height of 1,410 feet.

•

Michigan has the longest shoreline in the contiguous U.S.

•

There are five counties in Texas that are larger than the state of Rhode Island.

•

Coca Cola was banned from India in 1977 for refusing to disclose its secret formula.

•

Men are eight times more likely to be colorblind than women.

•

Of every 100 people in the world, 21 live in China. Five out of 100 live in the U.S.A.

•

The leading untreated illness in the U.S. is mental depression.

•

When he signed the statehood bills for North and South Dakota on the same day, President Benjamin Harrison wouldn't tell which one he signed first, so no one knows which is the 39th or 40th state.

GRAFFITI

HE WHO CARRIES TALE MAKES MONKEY OF SELF.

Nothing to sneeze at: American consumers spend more than a billion dollars a year on cold relief medicines.

•

Heart attacks claim the fewest men on Fridays.

•

Melt an ice cube in your mouth and you'll burn off 2.3 calories.

•

Mary Westmacott was the pen name of Agatha Christie when she was writing romantic novels.

•

In the "gimme some space" department: a "hairsbreadth away" is 1/48 of an inch.

•

Teflon was called "fluon" when it was first discovered in 1938.

•

Rats can swim half a mile and tread water for three days.

•

Mickey Mouse has four fingers on each hand.

•

Of Pluto the former planet and Pluto the canine, the Disney dog was named first.

GRAFFITI

ZEBRA iS 25 SiZES BiGGER THAN "A" BRA.

Olive Oyl's measurements are 19-19-19.

•

The most popular name for a pope is John. There have been 23 Pope Johns (25 if you count the two John Pauls).

•

Los Angeles is the second most populous Mexican city.

•

If you suffer from polydactylism, you have more than your fair share of fingers or toes.

•

Americans say their favorite color is blue, but the most popular car and house color is white.

•

According to Hoyle, poker is the national card game of the U.S.

•

Bela Lugosi is buried in his black Dracula cape.

•

One of Thomas Jefferson's many inventions was the swivel chair.

•

Andrew Jackson's pet parrot was in attendance at the former President's burial service, but was removed for screeching profanities.

QUICK QUIZ

Which one of The Seven Dwarfs was beardless?

Dopey.

George Washington, the "Father of Our Country," had no children.

•

The greyhound is the fastest dog in the world, clocked at 41.7 miles per hour.

•

According to an intelligence test of 79 dog breeds, the smartest is the Border collie.

•

In humans, the right lung weighs more than the left.

•

The most common noncontagious disease is tooth decay.

•

NFL coaching legend Vince Lombardi coined the phrase "game plan".

•

Attorneys and lawyers are not necessarily the same. Anyone can act on your behalf and be called your attorney, but to be called a lawyer, one must be a graduate of law school.

•

Olivia Newton-John got her start in show business when she won a Hayley Mills look-alike contest.

THOUGHTS OF THE THRONE

On average, the Pentagon uses 666 rolls of toilet paper in one day. As they say in government circles, no job's finished until the paperwork is done.

A cat's sense of smell is ten times better than a human's.

•

T.S. Eliot's favorite gift to critics was exploding cigars.

•

Listen up! About that ear that van Gogh cut off- it was his left one.

•

Benjamin Franklin owned the first bathtub in the colonies. Good thing he didn't try the lightning experiment there.

•

Cary Grant was expelled from school at age fourteen for sneaking into the girl's room.

•

Confucius was not always a famous philosopher. At age seventeen he was a corn inspector at the markets.

•

Kim Basinger, Raquel Welch, Dyan Cannon, Carly Simon and Steve Martin were all cheerleaders.

•

President Ulysses S. Grant was once arrested for exceeding the speed limit when driving a team of wild horses through the streets of Washington.

GRAFFITI

EARTHQUAKE PREDICTORS
ARE FAULT FINDERS.

Before getting into acting and directing, Sidney Poitier trained as a physiotherapist in a mental hospital.

•

The only state to have developed a distinct breed of dog is Maryland, with its Chesapeake Bay retriever.

•

Only 4% of comic book collectors are female.

•

The real name of Eddie, the scrappy dog on TV's *Frasier*, was Moose (who, at 16, died of old age in 2006).

•

In skywriting, the average letter is nearly two miles high.

•

62 out of 100 Americans say that the worst day of the week is- you guessed it- Monday.

•

The second man to walk on the lunar surface was Buzz Aldrin. His mother's maiden name is Moon.

•

Because his son-in-law was late with the carriage, Thomas Jefferson had to walk to his own inauguration.

GRAFFITI

"POLITICALLY CORRECT"
IS A CONTRADICTION IN TERMS.

The first President born in a hospital was Jimmy Carter.

•

For some unknown reason, a duck's quack doesn't echo.

•

According to a Gallup poll, the most hated food in America is liver.

•

Most trips taken in the U.S. by car are less than five miles.

•

Stainless steel can be rolled into strips thinner than human hair.

•

Tiny hairs on the feet of flies act like taste buds as they stroll over your food.

•

75% of optometrists wear eyeglasses.

•

Marietta, Ohio, is named for Marie Antoinette.

•

Every single pet hamster is a descendant from one female wild golden hamster found with a litter of 12 young in Syria in 1930.

•

An elephant grows six sets of teeth during a lifetime.

QUICK QUIZ

Who was the last Vice-President to become President of the United States?

George H.W. Bush.

During a game of jai alai, the speed of the ball can reach 160 miles per hour.

•

In 1976, twenty invited guests witnessed an official marriage ceremony between a Los Angeles secretary and a fifty-pound rock.

•

The ouija board's name comes from combining the French and German words for "yes".

•

The first Super Bowl given a Roman Numeral was IV.

•

Smokey Bear is the only one in America with his own zip code-20252.

•

Not to rain on your parade, but there are over one quadrillion ants living on the planet.

•

Ants will not cross a white chalk line.

•

The reaction time of a cockroach is 54/1000 of a second, so you best not get into a gunfight with one.

THOUGHTS OF THE THRONE

The majority of toilets flush in E flat.

When NBC plays three musical notes with its logo on TV, those notes are "G-E-C" for the General Electric Corporation, which owns the network.

•

17 million Americans suffer from triskaidekaphobia, the fear of the number 13.

•

One out of four Americans is superstitious.

•

According to a Gallup poll, 27% of Americans knock on wood.

•

Playing the piano can use up more calories than doing light exercise.

•

Last names in China are always one syllable.

•

Pepto Bismol, when introduced in 1901, was called Mixture Cholera Infantum.

•

Kodak camera inventor George Eastman hated to have his picture taken.

GRAFFITI

ADAM LOVED EVE - WHO ELSE?

A grasshopper's blood is white.

•

Eleanor Roosevelt's maiden name was Roosevelt.

•

If you're feeling sexdactyly, it means you have six fingers on each hand.

•

Onions can be stored for longer periods of time than any other vegetable.

•

If you had a line of dimes 113.6 miles long, you'd be a millionaire!

•

America's first billionaire was John D. Rockefeller, in 1911.

•

4% of San Francisco households are millionaires, the highest percentage of any city in America.

•

Bingo was originally called Beano.

•

Not long ago, a Bulgarian woman was allowed only one bath in her lifetime- and that was on the day before her wedding.

GRAFFITI

WHY ISN'T THERE A
MOUSE-FLAVORED CAT FOOD?

When National League umpire Tom Gorman died in 1986, he was buried in his blue umpire's suit, and with a ball and strike indicator in his hand. The count on it was 3-2.

•

At birth, a hippopotamus weighs about 100 pounds.

•

Buckingham Palace is the former site of a brothel.

•

Former baseball player Carlos May is the only big leaguer to have worn his birthday on his back. His number was 17, and his last name, which appeared above the number, read the same as the month in which he was born.

•

According to Hallmark, the month with the most birthdays is August.

•

The month with the fewest birthdays is- no surprise- February.

•

J. Edgar Hoover would not allow anyone to walk on his shadow.

•

Cows don't like spinach.

QUICK QUIZ

What's the score of a forfeited Major League Baseball game?

6-0

Wall Street's name stems from colonial times, when a wall was built around Lower Manhattan to protect cattle from Indian raids.

•

Albert Einstein was four years old before he could talk.

•

The average American adult male is 5 feet 9.1 inches tall. The average woman is 5 feet 3.7 inches tall.

•

The 1990 graduating class of the U.S. Navy's top school received diplomas stating they'd graduated from the Navel Academy.

•

If you're cynophobic, you have a fear of dogs.

•

1920 marked the first time the word "cheese" was used to encourage a smile. The Korean answer to "cheese" is "Kimchi" (pickled cabbage). In Spain, it's "Patata" (potato) and in China it's "Qiezi" (eggplant).

•

In 2005, the word "google" became an entry in *Merriam-Webster's Dictionary* as a transitional verb "to obtain information about on the World Wide Web."

THOUGHTS OF THE THRONE

Actress Jodie Foster put her Oscar
(Best Actress for her performance in *Silence of the Lambs*)
in her bathroom next to the tub.

The average age at which a baby begins to deliberately smile is eight weeks.

•

There are 2,598,960 different poker hands possible in a deck of cards.

•

You are twice as likely to get a heart attack in winter than summer.

•

Donald Duck's nieces are April, May and June.

•

Potato chips were invented in 1853 in Saratoga, New York, by George Crum.

•

There's a 1 in 4 chance that an American will eat at a fast-food restaurant on any given day.

•

According to *Fast Food Nation*, the average American eats three hamburgers each week.

•

The maximum number of letters on one line of a *Wheel of Fortune* game board is 13.

GRAFFITI

HE WHO CROSS COW WITH CRYSTAL BALL
GET MESSAGE FROM UDDER SIDE.

A group of owls is called a parliament.

•

There are 35 species of coconuts.

•

The soybean is the most versatile vegetable on earth, with over 400 different products made with it.

•

In 1990, the California legislature overturned a ruling that allowed dogs' teeth to be cleaned only by veterinarians.

•

The northernmost point in the contiguous U.S. is in Minnesota.

•

Snakes don't blink.

•

Charlotte Beysser Bartoldi was the model for the Statue of Liberty, which was sculpted by her son, Fredric Auguste Bartoldi.

•

The only U.S. landmark that's not stationary? The fabled cable cars in San Francisco.

•

Christopher Columbus had freckles.

GRAFFITI

NUDISTS SUFFER FROM
CLOTHES-TROPHOBIA.

Then and now: The average American used between 5 and 10 gallons of water a day in 1904. Today's American uses 100 gallons of water per day.

•

A tomato is 95% water.

•

97% of the earth's water is seawater.

•

John Adams, George Washington and Thomas Jefferson were avid marble collectors and players.

•

The Packard was the first car to cross the continent. It took 52 days in 1903.

•

Honeybees are deaf.

•

According to the Kleenex people, the average person blows his nose 256 times a year.

•

Something to chew on: As a public relations move, William Wrigley, Jr. sent 4 free sticks of gum to every person listed in the U.S. phone book in 1915.

QUICK QUIZ

Where would you typically find the letters
C, D, E, F, L, O, P, T and Z?

On an eye chart.

Every clown is unique. Their faces have to be painted on an eggshell to be registered. When a clown dies, his egg is buried with him, no doubt sunny-side up.

•

Gorillas can't swim.

•

The lobster automatically acquires a new form-fitting shell every year.

•

The most popular seafood in America is shrimp (topping tuna, which was the favorite until 2002).

•

Jay-Z was born Shawn Corey Carter.

•

The "J" in J. Edgar Hoover stands for John.

•

Ted Kennedy's middle name is Moore.

•

Starburst fruit chews were originally known as Opal Fruits.

•

The French call cotton candy "Papa's beard".

THOUGHTS OF THE THRONE

President William Howard Taft was the heaviest chief executive, tipping the scales at 325 pounds. After repeatedly getting stuck in the White House bathtub, he had one installed big enough to accommodate four average-sized men.

Sylvester Graham, a vegetarian who lectured on healthy diets, created graham crackers.

•

Washington, D.C., residents were not allowed to vote in presidential elections until the 23rd Amendment was ratified in 1961.

•

The name of the first presidential aircraft, in 1944, was Sacred Cow.

•

The U.S. President makes $400,000 a year; the Vice-President, $208,100.

•

Napoleon's hemorrhoids were a factor in his defeat at Waterloo. They kept him from being able to survey the battlefield on horseback.

•

Peter the Great personally cut the beards of all his noblemen.

•

Caesar and Napoleon were both epileptics.

•

Elephants can swim very well. They just have trouble keeping their trunks up.

GRAFFITI

MAN WHO EATS PHOTOGRAPH OF FATHER
BECOMES SPITTING IMAGE OF HIM.

Wild sheep don't bear wool.

•

The first edition of *The New York Times* appeared on September 18, 1851, and sold for a penny a pop.

•

The average American household watches 4 hours and 25 minutes of TV daily.

•

Lefthanders aren't allowed to play polo.

•

There are six and one-half million people in the U.S. who play tennis at least twice a week.

•

Most people put on their left sock first.

•

The four least used letters of the alphabet, in order of their infrequency, are Q, X, Z and J.

•

The male fox mates for life. If the female dies, he will remain single for the rest of his life. However, if the male dies, the female will find another mate.

THOUGHTS OF THE THRONE

Buckingham Palace has 78 bathrooms.
Apparently, the Queen likes a lot of thrones.

Street numbers in Japan are not assigned by the position of the house on the street, but by when the house was built. The older the house, the lower the street number, regardless of street location.

Seoul, the South Korean capital, simply means "the capital" in the language of the land.

•

Those symbols that cartoonists draw to replace epithets are called dingbats.

•

More than 90% of flowers have an unpleasant odor or no odor at all.

•

The "A&M" in Texas A&M stands for Agricultural and Mechanical.

•

On October 31, 1997, Violet Palmer became the first female NBA referee.

•

The king of hearts is the only king without a mustache in a deck of cards.

QUICK QUIZ

What's the name of the dog on the Cracker Jack box?

Bingo.

Charles Roser invented the Fig Newton.

•

548 peanuts are needed to make a 12-ounce jar of peanut butter.

•

Las Vegas is Spanish for "the meadows."

•

There are 118 ridges around a dime, 119 around a quarter.

•

In Japan, only 4% of the population is left-handed.

•

Elephants, when they've had one too many, can be terribly rowdy drunks.

•

Cabbage is 91% water.

•

3% of Americans hang family pictures in their bathrooms.

•

A mole can dig a 300-foot long tunnel in one night.

•

Tweety Pie was originally a pink canary, but censors complained that he looked naked, so his color was changed to yellow.

GRAFFITI

OBITUARY WRITERS HAVE THE LAST WORD.